Convict Nobbys

The story of the convict construction of Macquarie's Pier and the reconstruction of Nobbys Island

◇◇

Noel Davies

ISBN 978-1-4092-2383-2

Contents

Acknowledgements

◇◇

In mid-1992, while a mature age first year history undergraduate at The University of Newcastle, I was set a field exercise of researching a convict site in the Newcastle region. I chose Nobbys. I soon discovered that although there was a considerable amount of information available, it was contadictory and disseminated. From the point of deciding to write on the subject, on a part-time basis to bring this work to the point of publication, it has taken me over two years to collect and collate. During this time I have read dozens of books, journals and articles, all of which were the result of someone else's time and effort, effort for which I now have a greater appreciation. The repositories of my major sources were:

Archive Offices of New South Wales, Sydney
Auchmuty Library, University of Newcastle
Lake Macquarie Regional Public Library
Newcastle Regional Art Gallery
Newcastle Regional Public Library
Mitchell Library, Sydney

I would like to thank Dr J.W. Turner for his sound advice on the early drafts of this work, my daughter Angela Davies for providing her editorial expertise, and Jan Cummings for the excellent reproduction of charts.

Noel Davies

Introduction

On a clear summer's day, any observer standing on Nobbys Beach with their bare feet in the sand, enjoying the sensation of having the surf swirl around their ankles, would have difficulty imagining that the peaceful scenery of Nobbys and its environs could ever have been anything other than as it now appears — that is, an area that seems specifically created for their leisure. For generations, Nobbys has been a place where most Novocastrians have at sometime either promenaded, courted, surfed, fished or just simply enjoyed themselves in the sun. By unconscious consensus the residents of Newcastle have adopted Macquarie's Pier and Nobbys Island as the symbol of their region; and the island and the wall that stand so majestically at the mouth of the Hunter River serve Newcastle as silent sentinels, protectors of the gateway that leads to the riches of the Hunter Valley.

Tradition dictates that history must be romanticised and Australia's convict heritage has certainly been subject to that tradition. Newcastle, however, as an exclusive and brutal convict settlement, has failed to take its proper place amongst the more publicised and popular heritage venues that enjoy this tradition. One of the reasons for this absence of interest in Newcastle's rich convict heritage is because only vestiges of convict influence survive in Newcastle; yet despite this, the site of Macquarie's Pier and Nobbys Island not only survives but continues to flourish and render service to the community, just as efficiently as its builders from so long ago anticipated.

The construction of Macquarie's Pier and the reduction of Nobbys Island was one of the largest and most important projects in the colonial era of New South Wales, with the work proving to be a protracted and monumental task that effected the lives of the men and women of Newcastle for nearly 40 years. In the early part of the 19th century, events around Nobbys influenced the residents of Newcastle in a very different way than they do today, and for several decades the construction of the breakwater and the reshaping of the island profoundly affected the lives and fortunes of the people charged with the responsibility of planning and completing the projects.

Life in the early 1800s would not have been easy for anybody in the primitive little Coal River township, but at least for those in authority the projects represented a livelihood and the possibility of promotion; to the less fortunate convicts by whose labour the huge projects slowly proceeded, Macquarie's Pier and Nobbys Island represented something far more unpleasant. For the fettered felons assigned to the chain gang at the breakwater it was a place of servitude that meant deprivation and suffering that, if judged by today's standards and conditions, is difficult to imagine. The memories and experiences of these people, now so long departed, still permeate the foundations of an edifice that continues, in a practical way, to connect Novocastrians to the pioneers of their region.

There was never any complexity involved in the design of these immense colonial projects; in terms of engineering, Macquarie's Pier is literally an enormous wall of rocks strategically placed to protect the harbour from the sea, and although the projects lack the sophistication and architectural appeal of other more popular convict heritage venues in Australia, no other convict site attacks and tames nature in such a spectacular manner as does Nobbys Island and Macquarie's Pier. As wonderful as it would be to be able to view the story of the construction through the eyes of the convicts, this is difficult to do, for few records survive to aid or enable such a perspective, and as a consequence the reality of the era must be deciphered from the recorded reactions of bureaucrats.

Hopefully, this investigation will serve as an informative and accurate record of the building of the Breakwater and the reconstruction of Nobbys Island in the convict era, and at the same time encourage the inheritors of the region to appreciate the aspirations and sacrifices of those who established an important part of Australia's national heritage.

CHAPTER 1

Something About the Beginning

Captain James Cook

The discovery of Nobbys Island took place over 200 years ago. Who was the first European to sight Nobbys Island? He was probably just an ordinary seaman, a sailor on the *HMS Endeavour*. The moment was of no particular significance — why would it be? The island would have been just another high craggy rock protruding from what would seem to be an endless and hostile coastline. After a cursory four day call at Botany Bay, the *HMS Endeavour* weighed anchor on 6 May 1770 and had been tacking against a medium north-east wind, making slow progress up the eastern coast of New Holland; the *Endeavour* was homeward-bound for England via Batavia.

The first recording of the existence of the little island now so popularly known as 'Nobbys' was written into the ship's log on Thursday 10 May 1770 by the illustrious Captain James Cook:

> Noon — Gentle breeze and clear wea'r; the ext's of the land from N.41.E. to S.41' W., a small clump of an island lying close in shore, S. 82" W. Dist'ce of shore about 2 leagues. Lat'de obs'd, 32" 53'S.

Thus, with Cook's observation of an island not worth naming, began the recording of the Hunter Region's European history. Although Captain Cook would never know, he was the first seaman of the many thousands who would follow him and become part of an Australian maritime tradition — that of being positioned 'off Nobbys'.

The first chart on which Nobbys existence was recorded, although credited to Cook, was probably drawn by Isaac Smith (1752–1831). Smith, destined to become an Admiral in the British Navy, was a cousin of Cook's wife and had accompanied Cook on previous voyages. He had begun his career as a midshipman and had been trained

CAPE HAWKE
PORT STEPHENS
BROKEN BAY
PORT JACKSON
BOTANY BAY
CAPE BANKS
POINT SOLANDER

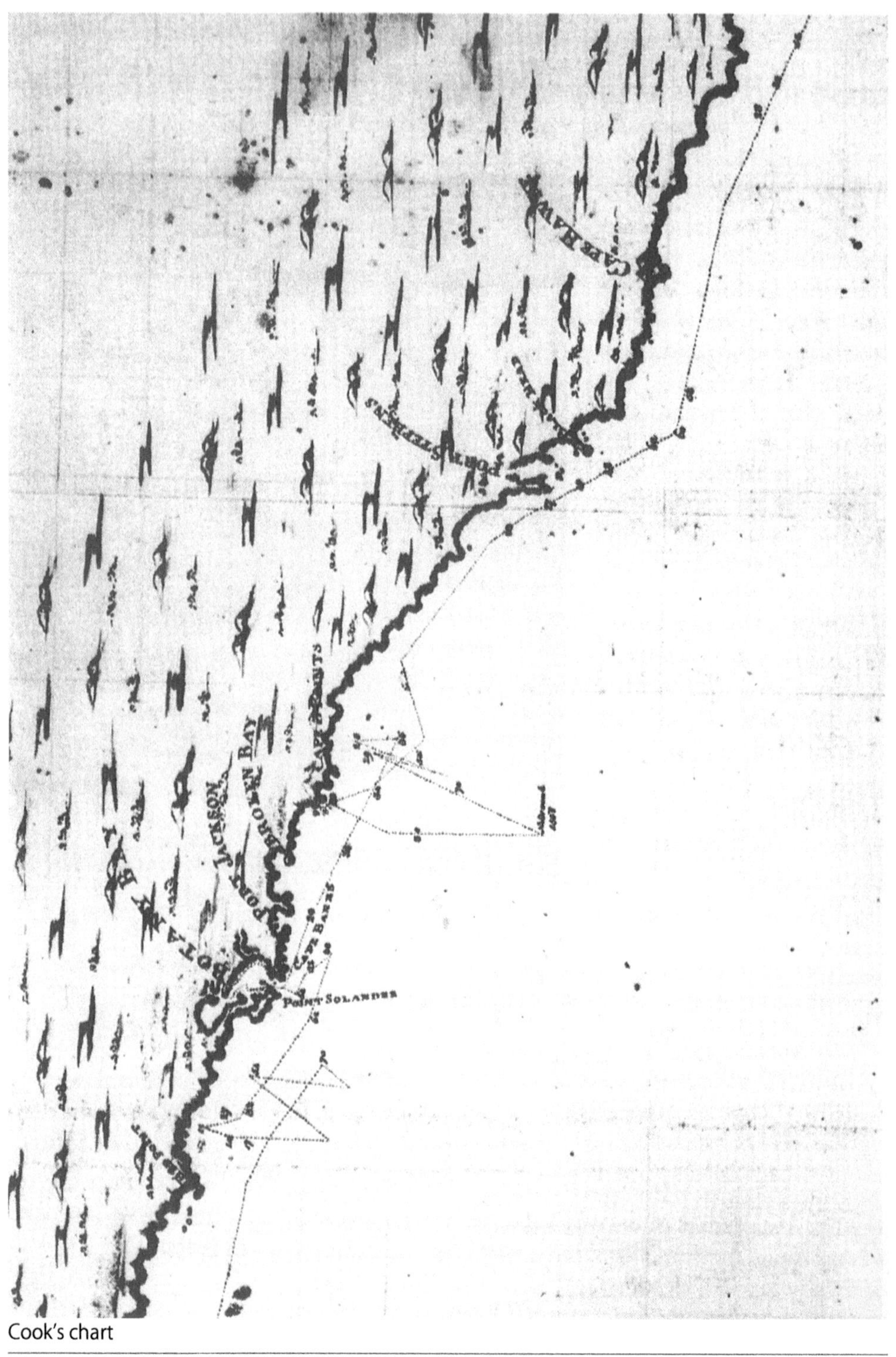

Cook's chart

through to cartographer by Cook., As the Captain's daily duties and responsibilities of running the ship would have been considerable, it is likely that Smith also took the sighting. Smith's claim to fame had already been established; it is reputed that at the historic first landing at Botany Bay, Cook tapped Smith on the shoulder and said, 'Isaac, you shall land first' and as a consequence, Smith became the first known European to set foot on the coast of New South Wales.

There has always been conjecture over who the first European to visit the Hunter River was. Anecdotal evidence suggests that others had visited the river before Lieutenant John Shortland discovered the region in 1797. The event that eventually brought about the official discovery of the Hunter River and its region occurred in September 1797. Twelve escaped convicts, mostly Irish and well led by a felon named Roberts, lured the small government vessel Cumberland to shore at Broken Bay. Here they overpowered the crew, put the coxswain and his three men ashore at Pittwater and then sailed away. The boat was never heard of again. There is some evidence to suggest that their escape from the isolated continent of Australia was one of the few that ever succeeded. It has been recorded that a notorious Cornwall smuggler named Roberts died in England in 1814, and just before his death he claimed that as a convict he had once escaped from Sydney by stealing a boat and making his way to England via Batavia.

The man charged with the responsibility to search north for the escapees was Lieutenant John Shortland (1769–1810) of the *HMS Reliance*. Lieutenant Shortland was a most resourceful naval career man; he had served on the *HMS Sirius* as a master's mate and like his father, (also named Lieutenant John Shortland) came to Australia as a 'First Fleeter' and was at the historic landing of Governor Phillip in Botany Bay in 1788.

Lieutenant John Shortland

Shortland was a man much admired for his sense of adventure and he was well-known for his daring stunts. For example, while stationed off Alexandria in 1803, Shortland flew a kite with a string attached over Pompey's Pillar, tied a rope to the string and then hauled the rope over the top. He then climbed the rope to the top of the pillar, a height of 160 feet, and there he drank a toast to the King's health. The next day he repeated the act and also added to the performance the eating of a beef steak.

Shortland searched as far as Port Stephens without finding any trace of the escapees and on 9 September 1797, while investigating the coast more closely on his return journey, he was drawn to inspect Nobbys Island. In doing so discovered the entrance to what is now called Port Hunter. Some say he was 'drawn by the beauty of the island', but it appears he was simply seeking temporary shelter. To Shortland, this was obviously a significant find; any discovery of a river was of extreme importance because a port means not only shelter for mariners, but the adjacent river also offers possible access to the interior. Shortland stayed a few days and made a rough survey of the harbour. He drew what he termed 'an eye sketch' and as was the practice of the day, named the various features of the harbour after his friends and benefactors. The only name that survives today is the Hunter River. Shortland actually called it Hunter's River, a dedication to the officer in command of the colony of New South Wales at that time. Governor John Hunter had also sailed to Australia with the First Fleet, serving as second in command to Governor Phillip. Hunter had been master of the *HMS Reliance* and Shortland had served under him in 1792.

What is now called Nobbys Island, Shortland named Hacking's Point after Henry Hacking, a noted local explorer. Hacking's Point seems a curious name for what was obviously an island, but no real explanation suggests itself. The southern headland now known as Fort Scratchley, Shortland named Braithwaite's Head, after Lieutenant Robert Braithwaite, and the northern point, now known as Stockton, he named Point Kent.

As the first European name of Nobbys Island was Hacking's Point, a small investigation of Henry Hacking makes an interesting story. Henry Hacking also came out to the colony with the first fleet in 1788 as the quartermaster of the *HMS Sirius*. He was 'reckoned a good shot', an observation that was certainly proven true when he claimed the dubious 'honour' of becoming the first man to shoot an Aborigine at Hunter's River in 1799 (in fact he shot three).

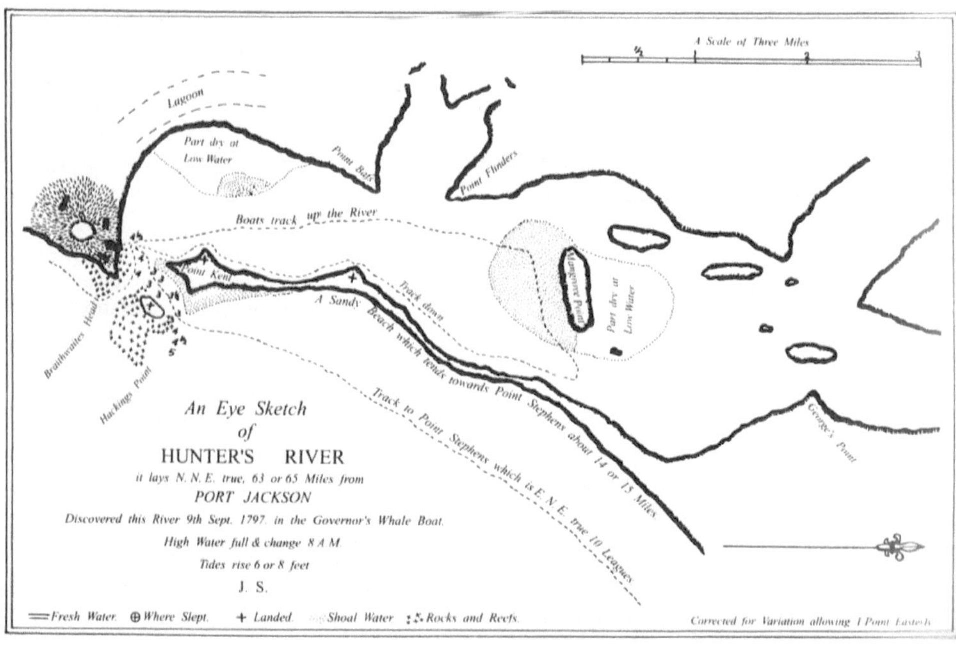

Hacking was a reasonably proficient explorer and pilot, but it seems that he had natural criminal tendencies and eventually he was caught stealing naval stores and sentenced to death. His sentence was commuted to penal servitude; but after serving six months in Van Diemen's Land he received a pardon. Hacking was then convicted for shooting a woman and once again sentenced to death. Governor King again pardoned Hacking saying, 'he is a good man but was lost here by the Arts of a Woman'. He died in Hobart an alcoholic at the age of 81 years, and is remembered as the discoverer of Port Hacking.

The discovery of the Hunter's River port, and of course Nobbys, does not seem to have been particularly noteworthy to the authorities and Shortland's career as a regional explorer was brief. Shortland returned to England in 1800 to continue his distinguished career in the Royal Navy. Lieutenant John Shortland was destined to die as he had lived, a professional navy sailor in the service of his country.

In 1810, aboard his ship the *Junon*, ironically a captured French vessel, he and his company were caught in the Atlantic by the French navy and immediately engaged in a desperate battle. Hopelessly outgunned by four French warships, Shortland gallantly directed the defence of his ship until half his crew were killed and himself severely wounded. After his capture, his ship was found to be so badly damaged from the one sided battle, it was not possible to salvage the ship, and as a consequence the *Junon* was burnt. Mortally injured, Lieutenant John Shortland was taken by his French captors to Guadeloupe Military Hospital where on 10 January 1810, the discoverer of Hunter's River died of his wounds.

After Shortland's report, the only visitors to the region before 1801, were the tough and enterprising Sydney traders that ventured up the coast in their small boats for the purpose of procuring coal and cedar, they called it the Coal River. Although history has it that Nobbys was substantially mined for coal, this is not so as the coal available 'just a musket shot away' on Colliers Point was more easily accessible and of a superior quality.

The officer who had accepted charge of the colony in 1800, Governor Phillip Gidley King, was impressed by the traders' endeavours (and probably their profits) and with the prospect of expanding the lucrative trade in coal and cedar, King organised a survey of the area to assess the viability of establishing a permanent settlement at the Coal Harbour (the name it had now acquired). Under the command of Lieutenant James Grant R.N., the brig *HM Lady Nelson* and the schooner *Francis* were dispatched to the Coal River. On board were Lieutenant-Colonel William Patterson, the officer charged with the responsibility of the expedition; Surgeon John Harris; Ensign Barrallier, an engineer and surveyor; J.W. Frewin, an artist; J.H. Platt, miner; Mr James, pilot; five sawyers; six soldiers; an Aborigine named Bungaree; and the crews of the vessels. The party of 70 arrived on 14 June 1801, anchoring under the lee of Coal Island (as Hacking's Point or Nobbys was then known).

The next morning Lieutenant Grant, accompanied by Mr Harris, left his vessel at 10.30 and rowed around Coal Island, landed on its shore, climbed to the top of the island and as a signal that the entrance to the river was safe, hoisted the Union Jack. This was to be the first flag of many that would be flown from Nobbys Island. The vessels were then towed into the harbour by their long-boats and moored close to the shore by securing them to nearby trees. There is an entry in Grant's journal stating that the location of the river was not obvious, and on the way up the coast he had actually mistaken the entrance to Lake Macquarie for that of the Hunter River. His journal entry of 14 June 1801, however, would prove most prophetic for Nobbys Island:

> Here I hoisted a Union Jack as a signal to the vessel that this was the right entrance of the river we were in search of I must remark that this Island is well calculated for defending the river's entrance, and the proper place for erecting a signal tower or lighthouse.

If Ensign Francis Luis Barrallier R.N. (1773–1853) is not remembered as the explorer who, while looking for a way across the Blue Mountains, was supposed to be the first European to discover the Aboriginal use of the bush call 'coo-ee', he will be remembered as the officer in charge of carrying out the first official survey of the Hunter's River. His original chart of Coal Harbour featuring Nobbys Island as Coal Island is now a historic document. As the survey progressed, the features of the harbour were renamed and although it can be established that Lieutenant-Colonel William Patterson (1755–1810) (the man destined amongst other things, to be wounded in a duel with John Macarthur), on 25 June 1801 officially changed the names Hacking's Island to Coal Island and Braithwaite's Head to Colliers Point, there is ample evidence suggesting that these two names must already have been colloquially established well before this date. The same situation occurs with the name Coal River and Coal Harbour. These names were probably simply coined by the traders that been using the area in the previous years.

The first real attempt at establishing the Coal River as an exclusive and isolated penal settlement began when three small vessels dropped anchor in the harbour on 30 March 1804. The contingent of 12 soldiers, 34 prisoners that were mostly made up from the Irish rebellion at Vinegar Hill, and four civilians; all ably led by a 21 year old enthusiastic volunteer Lieutenant Charles A.F.N. Menzies, the soldier who by coincidence or not, had commanded the guards that had put down the rebellion of the Irish at Vinegar Hill.

Governor King had commissioned Menzies as the 'Commandant and Magistrate of the settlement of Newcastle in the County of Northumberland' and it was Governor King who selected the name Newcastle. He wrote:

> Although the harbour and the river will still retain their original name, yet I have considered it advisable, to avoid future mistakes, to give the settlement a name, and none appears so applicable as that of Newcastle.

Obviously King equated the Coal River with the coal town of Newcastle-on-Tyne, Northumberland County, England. In truth, however, it was a simple fact that in colonial society of the early 1800s, very few people were much interested in the name or the happenings at Newcastle. Newcastle was to Sydney what Sydney was to London — 'The Camp' was a place you had to have, but absolutely not a subject fit for conversation in polite company.

History is rarely as it is depicted — its romantic portrayal always contains some truth. But the established myths that are preferred as history seldom match reality. In Newcastle in the early 1800s, over a relatively short period of time and without much provocation a man could receive hundreds of lashes from the dreaded 'cat-o-nine tails'. Often the floggers or 'scourgers' were part-time professionals and indeed the work must have been either extremely exhausting or unpopular, because to attract participants, the Colonial Secretary was forced on 1 January 1836 to raise their rates from nine pence to one shilling and nine pence per day of flogging.

The settlement of Newcastle was founded to serve as a direct instrument of the British colonial justice system. With severe penalties for relatively minor offences, it is not difficult to comprehend why there were so many capital convictions in the era. No less than 174 offences carried the death penalty, and yet some of the offences committed against the person that would be considered heinous today, were sometimes treated as trivial. For the lower classes of England, minor crime was considered more a way of life than as anti-social conduct, and in the complete absence of social services it remains difficult to condemn this culture of petty crime. It has been estimated that around the year 1800 one person in eight residing in London was involved in some kind of criminal activity.

To hang so many people would obviously be impractical and this practice was never as common as it is so often purported to be. More often than not, the alternative to hanging a convicted person for the more minor of capital crimes was to commute the death sentence to transportation. Contrary to current general belief, almost all of the convicts transported to Australian colonies were not the innocents whose image has been popularised by novels and film, but were usually multiple offenders and habitual minor criminals.

The Coal River settlement, as Newcastle was first known, was established for two specific purposes. First, as place to transport the transported; in other words, if convicts re-offended after arrival in the colony, they were sent to the Coal River settlement to isolate them even further from society, truly making Newcastle a 'city of thieves'. Secondly, Newcastle was settled to establish a government monopoly over the cedar and coal in the region. The abundant cedar stands and the quality coal that were so easily accessible at Hunter's River were considered a rich and immediate practical asset for the fledgling colony.

'The Camp' as Newcastle was known, was basically a primitive and totally restricted gaol. No person was allowed to enter or leave the penal settlement without express prior permission in writing from the Governor. If a ship entered the harbour without papers it could be confiscated or scuttled, if a sailor (even the Captain) was found ashore after dark, he could be summarily flogged. In the early days, basically only two types of people resided at 'The Camp', soldiers and criminals. For the intractable felons sent to Newcastle, the Coal River's reputation was no less damned than that of the infamous Norfolk Island or Van Diemen's Land. The different Commandants came and went, but the harsh conditions experienced by all at the settlement varied little. Newcastle was the place designated to punish contumacious prisoners and punish it did!

Living conditions in Newcastle in the early 1800s, when compared to Sydney, were for convict and soldier alike, very poor and most residents of Newcastle regardless of their status, considered themselves to be in transit, usually being desperate for a more comfortable life elsewhere.

By law the welfare of the prisoners was the responsibility of the Governor, and the government regulations laid down would seem to have been sufficient to ensure their survival. The regulation issue of clothing, or 'slops' as they were known, was two blankets, two shirts, two caps, four pairs of shoes, and two suits of woollen cloth per prisoner per year. The weekly allowance for food was eight pounds of wheat and seven pounds of salt pork or salt beef or salt mutton. Women received exactly half of the ration quantity of the men, children received one quarter. Unfortunately putting the responsibility for food and rations into the regulations did not necessarily guarantee their existence, and often food and clothing were delivered not only irregularly, but in

Some of the 'old crawlers' convicts of Port Arthur, 1874

poor condition as well. The acquisition of food and clothing was a constant source of contention in the settlement, and although severely punishable, the practice of trading for food and clothing, stealing goods, or exchanging sexual favours to obtain the basic essentials required to survive was continuous. It was this scenario that made the corruption of both the soldiers and the convicts not only rampant, but also inevitable.

On the word of an overseer anxious to be seen justifying his position as a trustee, or perhaps the trustee simply attempting to ingratiate himself with his superiors, a convict could be accused of almost anything by the trustee and be punished summarily and with little recourse. For example, insolence to a trustee would bring 25 lashes, a prisoner 'suspected of stealing carrots from the commandant's garden', 50 lashes, a convict absent from his work without permission, 'fifty lashes', abusive language, 50 lashes and so on. The punishment was carried out daily and witnessed by all. Apart from the daily deprivations with which the convict population of Newcastle had to contend, for all in the colony of New South Wales, life expectancy was much shorter than that of more modern times. Pro-rata, the incidence of accidents, violence and murder in colonial days was a great deal higher than it is in more modern times. The circumstances of death, especially for males, was more often than not, unnatural.

A sample of the Sydney Coroners Report for two weeks in March 1834 reflects the times:

John Sullivan	Accidentally Killed	Anne Flaerty	Found Drowned
Chris Ferguson	Visit by God	William Kitchen	Hanged
I. Chaplin	Accidentally Drowned	W Burns	Accidentally Killed
Rob Freeman	Found Drowned	George Wolly	Suffocation
Mrs Freeman	Found Drowned	Thomas Warwick	Accidentally Killed
I. McEvery	Found Drowned	Elizabeth Crawford	Accidentally Killed
A. Flaerty	Found Drowned	Thomas Smith	Wilful Murder
Sara Crozier	Found Drowned	A. Kitchen	Wilful Murder

As Australia's struggle and need to create its own ethos and mythology continues, it has been a natural reaction to condemn the behaviour of the bureaucrats and sympathise with the plight of the convicts. Basically driven by self-interest, society develops what it requires as the needs arise, and all of the players in Australia's primitive and brutal past were still strictly controlled by their own gradually changing society. Given the fact that Australia was basically a giant gaol, it is difficult to imagine how early circumstances for the emigrants could have been very much different than they were.

CHAPTER 2

Pre-History of Nobbys Island

The 200 years of European history in Australia represents but a breath in the life of the cut-down rock that we now know as Nobbys Island. It is said that some of the peculiarities of the Australian ethos are a result of the lack of a past with which Australians can identify, yet their recently adopted country has a cultural history which is unequalled in the world. Unfortunately, the history and significance of Nobbys Island to those occupying the region before the coming of the European settlers is not really known, but what is known, is that the area around Nobbys has been occupied by Aborigines for at least 8,000 years, and it is possible that ancestry of the local Aboriginals could go back as far as 40,000 years. As every part of an Aboriginal's landscape was an integral and spiritual part of their lives, the simple but majestic isolation of the island at the mouth of their river, separated from the mainland about 10,000 years ago, would surely have been of significance to their culture. Although nobody seems to know what the name means, it was recorded by the early European residents that the Aboriginals called the island *Why-bay Gamba*.

Although Aboriginals had developed a culture and way of life that for 40 millennium required little change to maintain their perspective of prosperity, the development of their civilisation was totally unrecognised or appreciated by the early European observers. Despite well meaning decrees that were designed and enacted by authorities to protect the interests of the natives, little government control over the soldiers, convicts and settlers was ever exercised. The local tribes were subjected to the usual abuses of shootings, abduction and rape of women and exposure to European disease, diseases which almost extinguished them altogether. Through ignorance, the cultural significance of the island and its area to the lives of the Awabakal and Worimi tribes was after 8,000 years, lost forever.

The shape of Nobbys Island that is so familiar today even to non-Novocastrians, is a far cry from the mass that it once was; the 200 million year old island was once much larger and was originally joined to the mainland. At its time of European discovery, the island's height was more than twice that of today. In 1801 the island was estimated by the engineer and qualified surveyor Ensign Francis Barrallier, to be 203 feet high. The shape of today's island bears no resemblance to that of yesteryear. With the Nobbys and Yard coal seams easily visible in the high rock strata, early drawings show that the island was formed like a high slice of a plum pudding, and in fact the island has been referred to as the 'pudding stone'. This work of nature that had survived for millions of years was destined to be reduced to a man made modern sculpture that somehow, even today, seems to represent what we know as civilisation.

CHAPTER 3

The Naming of the Island

Because the name 'Nobbys' seems in some way to simply infiltrate the history of Newcastle without any official re-naming of Coal Island, an investigation of how the name 'Nobbys Island' came into being is warranted. Although at the time of this publication, no material has been discovered that can positively substantiate the origin of the name, there are a number of theories on the subject which continue lively debate amongst Novocastrian historians.

The time frame in which the naming of the island fell was between 1804, when the name of the island was officially changed from Hacking's Point to Coal Island by Lieutenant-Colonel William Patterson, and 1810, the time of the first official recorded use of the name. It seems reasonable to assume that the almost anti-bureaucratic name, Nobbys, suggests that the title came from a colloquial source. Also the fact that the name originally contained an apostrophe suggests that the island may have been named after a personality.

The first written reference to Nobbys Island appeared in the *Sydney Gazette* on 6 October 1810 when the paper reported an account of the unfortunate deaths of William Wallis and William Radkin, two seamen from the ship Resource. They were drowned while on a fishing excursion just off the island.

The *Sydney Gazette* on that day reports:

> Last Sunday se'nnight a hurricane set in at Hunter River, which, it is feared, proved fatal to two of the seamen belonging to the Resource, then lying at the Coal Harbour. The two persons spoken of, whose names were William Wallis and William Radkin, had obtained the Master permission to go fishing in the vessel boat; and were off Nobby's Island when the gale commenced, which was about half-past 11 in the forenoon. They were driven off the land in a direction towards Port Steven, and seen from the vessel as far as the Sand-hills, when their boat disappeared. Part of her wreck has since been found ashore near Port Steven, but no vestage remained that

> could possibly favour the hope of the unfortunate men surviving; and to heighten the calamity, both leave families to deplore their untimely destiny.

Another name commonly used in the early 1800s was Booby Island, this name was recorded on a map drawn by a Lieutenant Cunningham in 1822. The most probable explanation for the name of Booby would be a connection with a sea bird belonging to the gannet species. A 'Booby' was also colloquial derogatory term for a weak willed and soft convict.

A strong theory is that from the sea, Signal Hill (Fort Scratchley) and the island were seen as landfall marks by the early visitors and called 'The Nobbies'. Lieutenant Shortland, the official discoverer of Port Hunter, is even reputed to have referred to the island as 'The Nob', and while returning to Sydney following his unsuccessful pursuit of escaped prisoners, is supposed to have been so struck by the beauty of The Nob that he ordered his crew to steer a course to allow him to observe the island more closely and thus he fortuitously discovered the harbour. However, no evidence exists to support this claim and historians assert that the reason he made for the lee of the island is that he was seeking temporary shelter.

Another theory on the origin of the island's name is that Nobbys is a misnomer for the island being named after a Lieutenant Thomas Hobby of the 102nd regiment. Perhaps Nobbys was a deliberate jest connected to Lieutenant Hobby's appearance? A more obscure idea suggested is that the original shape of the island was similar to a cocked hat and that there is a connection to the fact that in the 19th century a 'nobby' was a hatter's clerk.

Arguably, the most popularly accepted explanation of the origin of the name of the island by the community is that at one time a convict was supposed to have resided on the island, whether by choice or not is not known, named Joseph Nobby. Convict records do show that a Joseph Nobb arrived in the colony aboard the *Worcester* in 1802, but so far no record of his presence in Newcastle has surfaced.

There was a tradition in the armed services at the time, a tradition that still continues to be practiced today, of nick-naming any person named Clark or Clarke, 'Nobby'. The name Clark, however it was spelt, was an extremely common name in the convict era and there were many Clarks amongst the early not so voluntary residents of Newcastle. However, before 1810 there is no individual named Clark who could be specifically associated with the island.

While the official name for the breakwater is Macquarie's Pier and the once Nobbys Island is now Nobbys Signal Station, most local residents simply refer to the entire area as Nobbys, with no real distinction being made between the pier and the island. Any Novocastrian youngster could direct you to Nobbys or Nobbys Breakwater, but unfortunately for posterity a traveller risks a blank stare if they inquire about Macquarie's Pier.

There are many who have attempted to answer the question of the origin of the name Nobbys, and all have failed. Regardless of the reason that caused the island to be named Nobbys, the title has certainly met with the approval of the residents of Newcastle. Perhaps the mystery of the origin of the name Nobbys will remain unsolved and continue to provide popular conjecture and argument for Novocastrians forever.

CHAPTER 4

Macquarie's Pier

◇◇

It was Nobbys Island that featured in Lieutenant John Shortland's discovery of Coal Harbour, and although for many years the island would remain unchanged and continue to be the distinguishing landfall feature of the river entrance, and the navigational reference point by which ships could enter the harbour, it was initially to be the breakwater project alongside Nobbys Island that would be of more interest to the early residents of the town of Newcastle.

As with all history, there are always more questions than answers, and the study of the history of Macquarie's Pier is little different. There are two overriding questions about the construction of Macquarie's Pier that remain controversial and still affect people's perception of its history, yet this should not be so. The first question that appears unanswered is, 'whose idea was it to construct the breakwater?'. The second question is, 'when did the work begin?'.

Although there are various theories that persist in suggesting the possibility of an earlier beginning on the project other than the official day of 5 August 1818, primary sources reveal little evidence to suggest an exact date of the start of construction on the pier other than that of the time of the association of Commandant James Wallis and Governor Lachlan Macquarie.

Exactly where the original idea to construct the breakwater came from has never been established, but to any person concerned with the security of loading and mooring boats in the harbour, the idea of building a breakwater to negate the uncomfortable and dangerous harbour swell being generated by the outside sea would have been obvious. The continuation of the coal seams on Collier's Point (Fort Scratchley) from Coal Island (Nobbys) and the reef that connects the island and the headland show that Nobbys was at some stage, in pre-history, joined to the mainland. The possibility of using the connecting reef as the foundation for a breakwater would also have been apparent to any engineering mind.

One interesting contender for the title of being the originator of the breakwater scheme, was put forward by the famous colonial architect Francis Greenway (1777–1837). In the 1830s Greenway made a retrospective ambit claim on the Government for services that he alleged to have rendered to the colony in the past, services for which he had not been paid. Apparently Greenway had visited Newcastle sometime between 1814 and 1818 and he maintained that it was his suggestion that the harbour facility be improved by building a sea wall. While many of Greenway's superb architectural achievements survive today, there is no record, other than his own claim, of his being involved in the breakwater project.

Any reasonable analysis of the capacities of the various Commandants that participated in the establishment of Newcastle before the time of Captain James Wallis rules out the possibility of their participation in establishing or even initiating the breakwater project.

As some publications have perpetuated the notion that Lieutenant Thomas Scottowe was the initiator of the breakwater project, and due to the historical persistence of the idea of an earlier start having been made on the breakwater construction before 1818, an examination of the era of Lieutenant Scottowe is necessary. On 25 July 1811, Lieutenant Scottowe assumed command of the small penal settlement of Newcastle, and it was during his administration that Governor Macquarie, accompanied by his wife, paid the first of his three visits to Newcastle. Governor Macquarie sailed from Sydney on 4 November 1811 on an inspection tour to Van Diemen's Land. He then sailed to, and visited, Port Stephens and afterwards called at Newcastle, spending Christmas of 1811 in the little settlement, returning to Sydney on 5 January 1812. It was on this first visit to the settlement that Governor Macquarie first inspected the Newcastle region, and it seems that he was impressed with its potential. The visit was an occasion of such importance that a day was declared a holiday for all. Perhaps Governor Macquarie discussed the idea of the breakwater with Lieutenant Scottowe, but the fact remains that there was only a total convict population of 243 at the settlement, and they were well occupied at the coal mines, salt pans, lime kilns and cedar cutting gangs. Apart from the fact that there is no way an initiation of a project of this size could begin without consultation with Sydney, it is obvious that any attempt on a small scale would have been unrealistic. The allocation of human (convict) resources, was for the entire penal era, subject to contention and inquiry and the primary allocation of convict labour in Scottowe's time of command was directed at establishing self-sufficiency and producing marketable product. There is no evidence to support the theory that the construction of the breakwater was commenced by Lieutenant Scottowe.

Due to the problem of overcrowding at the Parramatta gaol and the closure of Norfolk Island, a decision was made in 1814 to expand the infamous secondary punishment settlement of Newcastle in order to take this excess of convicts and to also include the acceptance of general prisoners; that is, prisoners that were not necessarily second-offenders. At this time there were 209 prisoners registered at Newcastle.

Lieutenant Thomas Thompson of the 46th Regiment succeeded Lieutenant Scottowe, and was the Commandant of Newcastle from 19 February 1814 to 30 June 1816. Captain James Wallis succeeded Lieutenant Thompson and it was in Captain Wallis' time that the construction of the breakwater was begun.

Probably the most unlikely use of the island in its history occurred under Captain Wallis' command. It has been suggested that the name Nobbys originated from a prisoner named 'Nobby' having been isolated on the island sometime before 1810, and indeed it was Captain Wallis who first thought of the idea of using the island as a special repository for convicts. Sometime in 1816, he marooned on the island, forty or so of the most refractory and unruly women of the settlement.

How to control female prisoners was a continuous problem for the commandants of all penal settlements in the colony. The commandants saw their problems concerning female prisoners in simplistic terms: how to provide work and gainfully utilise their labour, how to carry out punishment without the appearance of the complete brutality which was so acceptable for male convicts, and most vexing of all, how to contain the perpetual problem of the spreading of venereal disease. Keeping the men from the un-attached women proved to be impossible. Nearly all female prisoners were automatically regarded by the authorities as prostitutes, an undeserved reputation considering that in order to survive in the primitive and violent male-dominated society, women were left little choice but to acquiesce to the advances of those that could ensure their survival. Their desperate position was readily taken advantage of by the officers, soldiers and overseers and convicts. With literally no sway or representation in society, life for women prisoners in the primitive penal society of Australia was appalling. This offensive part of Australian colonial history is not well-documented and has never been properly researched.

Colloquial history has it that Captain Wallis left the women on the island completely unsupervised and subject to their own devices, charging them with the task of making clothes for convicts. It is said that at night the pathetic lamentations of the women could be clearly heard across the still waters of the harbour, and that many of the women perished or drowned themselves in despair. The tale is now part of the folklore of Nobbys Island, and although it may be possible to accept that the event actually took place, there is no evidence to suggest it lasted for very long, and the unfortunate affair does seem at odds with the management practices of Captain Wallis.

Evidence concerning the circumstances and dates affecting the beginning of the breakwater are confusing. Captain Wallis was probably the person that officially suggested the idea of building the breakwater, but even during Captain Wallis' time there is no evidence to suggest that the breakwater was started before Wednesday 5 August 1818, the official dedication day, nor is there any evidence in early colonial correspondence, paintings, drawings or engravings that the breakwater was commenced before this date.

Naturally there would have had to have been some preparation at the foreshore before Governor Macquarie's dedication ceremony, suggesting that there must have been some dialogue or correspondence between Governor Macquarie and Wallis beforehand, yet no such evidence survives other than an entry from Governor Macquarie's journal, dated 4 August 1818, the day before the opening ceremony. It states:

> At 1 p.m. I went along with Captain Wallis to look at and examine the channel dividing Coal Island from the South Head of Newcastle harbour, with a view to filling it up entirely by constructing a strong causeway between the island and the mainland for the purpose of deepening the harbour. We landed on the Island and sounded the channel between it and the South Head which does not exceed 7ft. in depth at low water and only about a quarter mile in breadth. After examining both sides of the channel, it was finally determined to commence forthwith filling it up by constructing a strong causeway of 30 ft. broad.

No doubt Governor Macquarie was aware of the precarious safety for moored vessels in the harbour, as already the government brig Elizabeth Henrietta, named after his pretty wife Elizabeth, and was the very boat in which they both arrived had some time in 1816, been overturned by the force of the breaking seas forging through the gap between Nobbys Island and Colliers Point. The disaster cost the lives of Captain Ross and an able seaman named Fitzgerald.

Governor Lachlan Macquarie

Whether or not Captain Wallis had a convict stonemason burn the midnight oil in order to make ready the foundation stone, or whether the idea was not so spontaneous, may never be known, but officially, the history of the construction of the breakwater began with the laying of the foundation stone by Governor Macquarie at 4 p.m. on 5 August 1818. Following the time-honoured tradition and established bureaucratic procedure used to secure support for a venture and ensure personal promotion, Governor Macquarie had the honour of accepting Captain Wallis' suggestion that the project be named 'Macquarie's Pier'. It seems that as effective a Governor as he was, Macquarie was certainly not averse to having himself commemorated at every opportunity.

On 5 August 1818 Macquarie wrote in his diary:

> At 4 p.m., accompanied by Captain Wallis, the Rev. Mr Cowper, Major Antill, Lieutenant Macquarie and Mr Meehan, I went to the shore of the channel dividing Coal Island from the South Head for the purpose of laying the foundation and first stone of the causeway or pier to be constructed across from the mainland to the island, and

> the stone being cut and ready with an inscription, it was accordingly laid with all due form in the presence of the artificers and labourers to be employed in the construction and Captain Wallis, having proposed that it bear my name, it was accordingly called after me, Macquarie Pier, which the present year 1818 was cut and enscribed on the foundation stone. After the foundation stone had been laid, the artificers and labourers were served with an allowance of spirits to drink success to the undertaking which they did with 3 hearty cheers. On my return home I called at the provision store I inspected it and found it in good order and well supplied with provisions. I also called at the watch on the beach recently erected by Capt Wallis and was much pleased with the neatness and appearance of it. We then returned home to dinner at 5. o'clock well pleased with my day's work.

In those days, a pier could be made of wood, but a stone-constructed sea wall was often called a 'mole' and in his correspondence Macquarie often referred to the breakwater as 'the mole'. In the first years of the construction the name 'Macquarie's Pier' was always used, but in later years, as Macquarie's persona became less familiar, the project was usually referred to as 'the breakwater'.

The foundation stone, which is popularly depicted with a pillar approximately six to eight feet high on top, is clearly shown in sketches from the era. In each case the pillar is shown to be situated at least one third of the way out to the island, and on the right hand side of the breakwater. To facilitate this, either the work would have to have been commenced at least 18 months before the foundation stone ceremony, or the stone was moved to this position later. It is possible that due to the rough nature of the work, and given the fact that unsubstantiated claims have been made that up to 400 men at a time worked on the project, that the stone was removed for safe-keeping during the construction; perhaps it was moved more than once? Although the convict construction time of the wall was spread over 28 years, the only surviving pictures that show the pillar in place are pictures that show a complete structure. Many drawings show another pole exactly opposite the pillar on the other side of the breakwater, with one sketch showing a structure joining them together. It seems there has always been a fabrication for some unknown purpose at this point on the breakwater ever since the completion of the project.

The fact that the construction took 28 years to complete makes it hard to believe that the pillar so often featured is from Macquarie's time, or if indeed the original foundation stone was incorporated in the popularly depicted pillar at all. More drawings of the breakwater exist without the pillar being shown, than with. One possibility is that the stone pillar shown was never connected to the foundation stone at all, but was some sort of harbour navigational aid. Unfortunately there does not seem to be any description or even a vague reference to the foundation stone in any historical document other than Macquarie's own journal. Logic dictates that if the decision to start the project was only made the day before the dedication ceremony, then the original fabrication of the foundation stone could not have been very elaborate and the

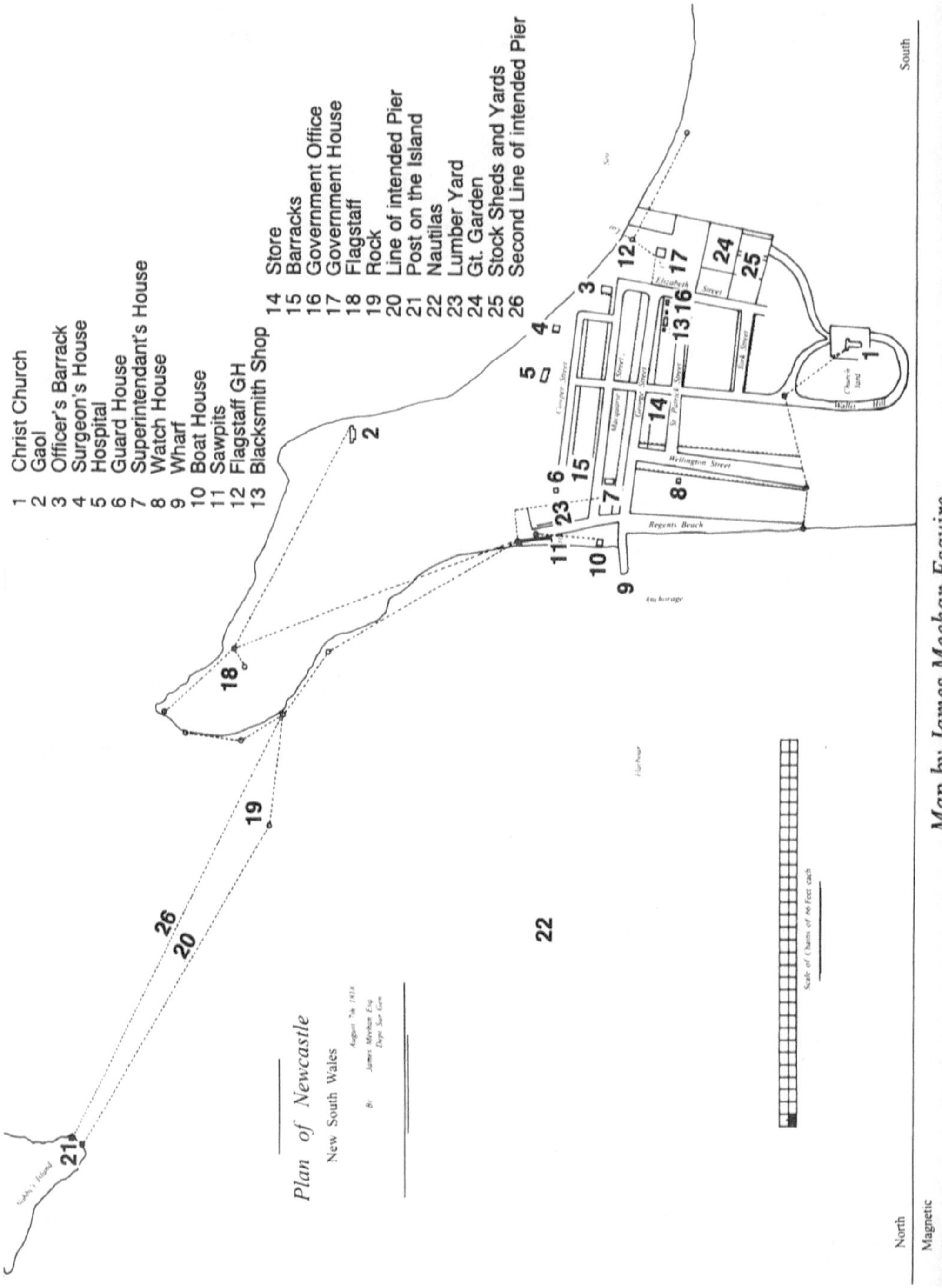

Plan of Newcastle

New South Wales

August 7th 1818

By James Meehan Esq
Dept Sur Gen

1 Christ Church
2 Gaol
3 Officer's Barrack
4 Surgeon's House
5 Hospital
6 Guard House
7 Superintendant's House
8 Watch House
9 Wharf
10 Boat House
11 Sawpits
12 Flagstaff GH
13 Blacksmith Shop
14 Store
15 Barracks
16 Government Office
17 Government House
18 Flagstaff
19 Rock
20 Line of intended Pier
21 Post on the Island
22 Nautilas
23 Lumber Yard
24 Gt. Garden
25 Stock Sheds and Yards
26 Second Line of intended Pier

Scale of Chains of 66 Feet each

North

Magnetic

South

Map by James Meehan Esquire

idea of a relatively ornate pillar is suspect. As a consequence of the lack of evidence, the existence and shape of the foundation stone will remain contentious, but somehow it feels right to think of the original stone still being safely buried somewhere in the structure.

Captain James Wallis was an expert artist and keen historian and produced one of the first books written about the colony of New South Wales (published in London in 1821). The work is entitled *Captain Wallis's Most Interesting and Historical Account of New South Wales and Its Settlements* and an original copy is housed in the University of Newcastle library. It is possible to comprehend the apathy associated with the subject of Newcastle in the early 1800s when considering that even Captain Wallis, Newcastle's own Commandant, completely ignored, in his own fine work, the discovery of the Hunter Region and the establishment of the penal settlement. An engraving of one Wallis' drawings has survived and includes a view of Nobbys which shows a substantial appendage to Collier's Point. This could be construed as the start of the breakwater project or simply some exposed rocks. The paper on which the picture was drawn is watermarked 1816, and probably forms the basis of the theory of an earlier start to the work on the wall by Wallis, but as the paper could have been used at any time after 1816, it hardly represents a convincing argument.

An accurate map of the streets and foreshores of Newcastle drawn on 7 August 1818 by a member of Macquarie's party, James Meehan Esq (1774–1826) clearly shows that a structure did not exist on Collier's Point before the official ceremony. (Note the numbers 20 and 26 on his map locating the intended pier line.)

The case of James Meehan is an excellent example of how Macquarie exercised his emancipative outlook. As a victim of an Irish political purge, on non-specific charges, Meehan had been transported to the colony by the British. Macquarie saw these charges as minor, and though still a convict, in 1812 Meehan was appointed by Macquarie as Deputy to the Surveyor-General and explorer, John Oxley. As officer in charge of all colony roads, bridges and streets, Meehan often accompanied Macquarie on his inspection sojourns. Meehan was familiar with the region because he had visited the Hunter River in 1801 with the then Surveyor-General, Charles Grimes.

With Governor Macquarie's blessing, and under the command of Captain Wallis, the breakwater rapidly progressed. As previously stated, there have been claims made by historians that as many as 400 convicts were allocated to the work, but surviving Quarterly Returns reports refute this. A report dated December 1819 records that 60 men were employed on the wall construction, and despite the fact that the project now enjoyed Macquarie's full patronage, the project would still not have demanded the high priority of utilising 400 men. Further supporting this argument is the evidence given in the comprehensive *Bigge Report* carried out between 1819 and 1821. His report showed that in that time of maximum convict population, the largest work gang in the settlement consisted of 256 men, and this gang was employed in the lumber yard.

Contrary to popular belief, construction methods on the breakwater were far from primitive. Cranes were used, one large one near the cliff face and two smaller ones at the end of the wall. A drawing from Sir William Dixson's collection, drawn by an anonymous artist and dated 20 January 1820, clearly shows the use of these three cranes and how that at this stage in the construction the stone was placed and correctly battered, not simply tipped. The original drawing is very fine and appears to show approximately 30 men working around the cranes.

Most of the breakwater gang were housed in close proximity to the project in, or by, the gaol. At this time Newcastle was taking 'short timers'; that is, men that were not necessarily hardened criminals serving long sentences. It has always been suggested that for the convicts of Newcastle, the task of lime burning was the most unpopular work allocation, but the most incorrigible characters were still usually assigned to the 'chain gang' to endure what was the most arduous and dangerous task in the settlement;

Sir William Dixson Collection, 1820, artist unknown

that of working on the breakwater. Basically, the breakwater prisoners were split into two groups — those employed in the quarry using pickaxes, hammers and wedges to cut stone, and those handling the stones on the breakwater itself.

Due to the proximity of the sea and therefore possibility of escape, all new arrivals allocated to the breakwater gang were chained and fettered until they had earned some degree of trust. As their movements were severely restricted by their fetters, the new arrivals were employed in cutting stone and attending the cranes. The prime time for work on the breakwater itself was at low tide and in fine conditions, but the men were still forced to work in all weathers. The official working hours for the convicts of the settlement varied. Some were 'tasked'; so many tons of coal mined or logs cut per man per day, but the hours worked by most were, in the winter months, eight hours per day Monday to Friday, five hours on Saturday, with Sunday left free (excepting for the compulsory attendance of the church service to ensure the salvation of their souls); in the summer months the weekdays were extended to ten hours of work per day.

Employment on the pier was wet and dangerous and death on the breakwater probably would not have been uncommon. Managing the huge stones with ropes and wooden derricks in the face of heavy seas was difficult and precarious work and would surely have been the cause of frequent accidents. Unfortunately, the accident rate of prisoners was not a statistic that afforded much interest to the authorities and they largely went unrecorded. Drownings in the colony were remarkably frequent.

James Morisset as a 16 year old ensign

On 1 January 1819, Captain James Morisset took command of the expanding settlement. Construction of the breakwater from the period beginning 5 August 1818 under Captain Wallis and subsequently to early 1823 under the now Major Morisset, was the most active and progressive period in the entire 28 year history of convict construction. Morisset was Newcastle's longest serving commandant, staying in the office for five years. Because more correspondence survives from Major Morisset's command than any other, Morisset has certainly generated the greatest amount of interest in the history of convictism in Newcastle. It is because of the availability of these records, and the fact that his term saw over 1,000 convicts housed at Newcastle that Morisset, of all the Commandants of Newcastle, became the most controversial. Only one official picture of Morisset exists, and this is a miniature painted when he was a 16 year old ensign. It is said that because Morisset was so badly facially disfigured, reputedly by a sabre cut received while serving under Wellington against the French in the Peninsular War, that he would not allow his likeness to be penned.

As his impressive war record and rapid promotion attests, there is little doubt about his bravery and ability. Although it is not difficult to show that many of Newcastle's commandants were much more brutal than Morisset, his historical image is that of an extreme disciplinarian. But then again, who today is qualified to judge the actions of those held responsible for establishing law and order in this, one of the most primitive and brutal societies? Morisset is known to have been an extremely able and productive commandant, and under his management, progress not only on the breakwater but indeed in the entire settlement was substantial. After the transference of the bulk of the Newcastle convicts to the new Port Macquarie gaol in 1823, the well salaried officer (£863 per annum) Major Morisset was replaced in November 1823 by Captain Gillman, a more junior officer who enjoyed a salary of only £160.

Although the breakwater was singularly the largest and most ambitious of the public works projects in the Hunter District, or for that matter, in the entire colony, at no stage did its construction generate the interest of other projects that affected the townspeople's welfare and lives with more immediacy. It is possible, as a consequence of this indifference towards the project, that there is almost no information available from the surviving records of this period. Morisset's quarterly returns showed progress at the breakwater to be 385 feet by 1 January 1820 and 625 feet 12 months later.

At least Governor Macquarie, during his long term, maintained a keen interest in the life and times of the pier bearing his name. He recorded in his daily journal on 29 November 1821, during his third and last visit to Newcastle, his pleasure in observing the progress:

> The grand pier or mole (named Macquarie Pier) I was rejoiced on inspection is now about half completed across the channel which separates Coal Island or Nobby, from the mainland on which the town of Newcastle is situated This channel is half a mile across. This pier is a noble and most important piece of work, but a most arduous and Herculean undertaking. It was commenced by Captain Wallis three years ago, and it will most likely take two years more to complete it. When this is done, however, the harbour of Newcastle will be both safe and commodious, and fit to receive ships of 500 tons burthen. Indeed the good effects of the pier is already felt, as it has already rendered the harbour secure, and deepened considerably the channel by which vessels must enter. The wreck of the Nautilus has been removed from where it choked up one side of the channel, in consequence of the force of the river current and freshes being confined to the principal channel by the erection of the pier.

There is no question that even though Captain Wallis's reason for naming the breakwater after Governor Macquarie was somewhat self-serving, Governor Macquarie's genuine interest and patronage of the breakwater was of enormous benefit to the project, and ultimately, to the settlement at large.

Although at the time Major Morisset was Newcastle's Commandant, on 4 November 1821, Governor Macquarie appointed Lieutenant Edward C. Close, at the princely remuneration of five shillings a day, to assist with the town's public works. Lieutenant Close was commissioned to build a small seven-gun fort and a coal fired beacon on Signal Hill (Colliers Point). The beacon was to be in continual operation for the next 36 years. Lieutenant Close also erected a hut of a peculiar shape near the beacon that was known as the 'pagoda'. As he was the appointed officer in charge of Newcastle's public works, the responsibility of improving Newcastle's harbour facilities, including the building and maintenance of the breakwater, fell within his portfolio of responsibilities.

One of the greatest political upheavals in Australian history affecting the future of Australia as a British colony, as well as the progress of the Newcastle's breakwater during the early period of its construction, was the inquiry conducted in 1819 by the Honourable J.T. Bigge.

Australian society had begun to develop in its own unique way, and much of this development was as a direct result of the emancipative policies of Governor Macquarie. As severe and restrictive as convict life in the colony appears, outside specific places of punishment like Newcastle, Macquarie's reformative policies and programs gave convicts a genuine chance to rehabilitate themselves and gain opportunity for early release. Macquarie rewarded convicts of good behaviour with shortened sentences, tickets of leave, conditional pardons and most importantly, land grants. Macquarie genuinely sought to achieve equality and self-esteem for the emancipated prisoners within the colonial community. His liberal philosophies and actions brought savage criticism of both the Government and his progressive methods of reform. The main censure came from two groups, the first being the local 'exclusives', a group of men that were wealthy landholders and businessmen. The second group was that of the London clique of colonial 'do-gooders'; that is, people that were interested in English overseas social policies — men with the ears of members of the House of Commons.

The elite minority group of squatters, politicians and businessmen, all ably led by the influential John Macarthur (1767–1834) of Merino sheep fame, with the availability of cheap land and free convict labour, had rapidly accumulated great personal wealth. These men saw their landholding empires being challenged by the immigrants and emancipated prisoners, and it was because of this threat that they continually lobbied the London authorities to curtail Macquarie's liberal actions of fostering opportunity and equality in the colony. The 'exclusives' openly accused Macquarie of self-aggrandisement by way of pointing out his obsession with massive public works programs, such as Macquarie Pier.

Not often mentioned in the succession of early Governors, ultimately to whom all responsibilities fell, is their appalling performance in condoning the dreadful treatment of the Aboriginal race. While on this issue Governor Macquarie was no better or worse than others, it cannot be denied that he tacitly supported the organised destruction of the Aboriginal race by the soldiers and settlers. But balanced against this shame, white history has since justly applauded Governor Macquarie's farsighted pastoral policies, his policy of granting early emancipation for deserving prisoners, and the heritage of the fine public works that he initiated. However, at the time, the factions both in England and Australia that did not concur with his progressive methodology proved to be extremely influential.

The man appointed to carry out the investigation was a 40 year old, experienced British magistrate, the Honourable John T. Bigge. Bigge arrived in the colony virtually unannounced aboard the *John Barry* on 26 September 1819, and to Governor

Macquarie's embarrassment, Bigge as a 'Commissioner of the Crown', carried unlimited powers of inquiry and was charged with the duty of investigating the affairs of the leading citizens and officials of the colony regardless of 'however exalted in rank or sacred in character they be'. The management of Australian government had never before, and has never since, been subjected to such scrutiny. The results of his findings took nearly three years to collate and publish, and while technically correct, basically reflected and sympathised with the opinion in London that Australia was not being governed in a way severe enough to suit their original prime objectives. That is, life in the colony was not capable of deterring criminals from offending in Britain.

As he did with all the major settlements in the colony, Bigge actually conducted his investigations on site. He arrived in Newcastle in January 1820 on HM Brig *Charlotte*, incidentally, the first ship built in Newcastle. Bigge conducted an exhaustive inquiry into all aspects of the community and, although not of primary concern, his inquiry included an investigation into the allocation of convicts to, and the purpose of, the construction of the breakwater. The thrust of Bigge's report was to save money by removing convicts from government service and placing them in private service.

Based on the comprehensive *Bigge Report*, a decision was made by the Colonial Office to curtail many of Macquarie's policies. Governor Macquarie had proffered his resignation to the Colonial Office three times during this period of controversy; it was finally accepted. By the time the *Bigge Report* was released, recommending that the colony return to a more severe penal philosophy, Macquarie had departed for Scotland and had been replaced by Governor Brisbane, saving embarrassment for both the government and Macquarie. Accompanied by his family, Macquarie returned to Mull, Scotland to make his home at the Jarvisfield (named after his first wife) family estate.

From that time on, the normally energetic and amicable Macquarie suffered from depression and poor health. Whether or not it was because of the Bigge affair is not really known, but it was while he was in London finalising his colonial affairs that he was suddenly taken ill. On 1 July 1824, attended by his devoted wife Elizabeth, the man most singularly responsible for the construction of the breakwater at Newcastle, died. His family tomb in Mull, is maintained by the National Trust of Australia. Governor Macquarie was responsible for leaving behind a colonial legacy that, from a white perspective, has never been equalled by another individual in Australia's history, and few men have contributed towards Australia's national identity as did Governor Lachlan Macquarie.

The newly appointed Governor Brisbane visited Newcastle on 4 January 1823, and whether or not the results of the *Bigge Report* also influenced his thinking, or whether the future benefits and original purpose of the breakwater project were simply beyond his comprehension, on 31 January 1823 Governor Brisbane's orders arrived; they instructed Commandant Major James Morisset to stop work on the breakwater altogether. The breakwater convict labour was re-allocated to what was perceived to be more productive pursuits such as roads and settler assignment. The breakwater project was officially abandoned on 31 January 1823 with 950 feet of the pier completed at the substantial cost of £25,000.

The Hon John T. Bigge

Following the removal of most of Newcastle's prisoners to the new, and even more remote, settlement of Port Macquarie and bowing to outside pressure to completely open up the fertile Hunter Region, on 3 March 1824 the penal settlement of Newcastle was declared available to all free settlers and emancipated convicts. The officer that established Port Macquarie as Newcastle's replacement place of servitude, was Newcastle's last Commandant, Captain Francis Allman (1780–1860). His office was officially abolished in June 1827.

These first few years of progress on the breakwater project were the most positive in what would now prove to be an extremely protracted project. The next stage of the construction of the breakwater would be associated with the cutting down and virtual desecration of Nobbys island.

Pre-historically, Nobbys Island and the mainland had been geographically bound, and with the arrival of the European pioneers, they were destined to be so once again. In the early days of Port Hunter, Nobbys Island was a separate entity to the mainland, and affected the life of the harbour in its own way, but after Governor Macquarie's and Captain Wallis' decision to secure the harbour from the sea by joining Collier's Point to Nobby's Island with a breakwater, the island and the pier were thereafter usually considered to be one environment.

CHAPTER 5

The Island and the Wall

No road yet existed between Newcastle and Sydney, so naturally the only access to the settlement was by sea. Before the completion of the breakwater and the subsequent improvements in the harbour signalling systems, even experienced mariners approaching the Hunter River port by sea in anything other than perfect conditions, considered the entrance extremely dangerous. An excerpt from Ensign Barrallier's letter to Governor King, dated 24 June 1801, gives an early seaman's perspective of the hazards of entering the harbour in a small ship, and at the same time brings to life the emotions of men from the past who have been 'off Nobbys' — from his writing it is clear that the passage he was referring to, was on the northern side of the island.

> You will see from my map what a dreadfully difficult crossing needs to be made in order to reach this beautiful river. The roaring of the waves which, hurling themselves one upon the other and breaking with afrightening din on the steep rocks of the island, and impetuously rolling along the sands of the opposite banks would fill the most intrepid seaman with trembling fear. You would have seen all the sailors with terror imprinted on their faces, but remaining steadfastly at their posts, obeying their Captain's commands with extraordinary dexterity so as to bring him through this almost impenetrable labyrinth.

In 1801, the distance between Collier's Point (Fort Scratchley) and Point Kent (Stockton) when viewed from the sea would have seemed wide, but as the few mariners that were familiar with the entrance to the harbour knew, the spoils of the Hunter were well protected by an almost continuous line of hidden reefs and shoals. Before the initiation of the breakwater project, there was a channel close to Colliers Point which could be used in good conditions; however, the main and safest entry from the sea to the port of Newcastle was between Nobbys Island and Point Kent (Stockton). In the days of sail the most controversial subject surrounding Nobbys Island was that of the island's effect on the safety of vessels attempting to enter the harbour in adverse wind conditions, and the difficult task of manoeuvring a large vessel under sail through this comparatively narrow and hazardous channel. As stated previously, the height of the island, at 203 feet, was over twice the height it is now; the mast heights of even the largest ships were rarely over 100 feet, with most masts being under 60 feet. As the approach of a vessel entering the harbour was governed by the direction of the wind, tide and the positions of shoals, mariners often found themselves becalmed behind the island and drifting without steerage towards the dangerous Point Kent banks. A common practice for ships arriving 'off Nobbys', was for the skipper to anchor his vessel in the lee of the island to await a favourable wind and tide that would allow the ship a safe entry to the harbour. If the ship was caught stationary by a storm and the anchor failed to hold the sandy bottom, the ship could easily drift onto the shoals or what is now Stockton Beach — many a good life and vessel has been lost this way.

The circumstances leading to the decision to cut Nobbys Island down is an integral part of the breakwater's history, and the latter stage of the cutting down of the island has become one of the region's great stories, but before the second stage of construction on the breakwater and the reshaping of Nobby's Island was instigated, there was a 13 year period of dormancy on the breakwater project.

A view of 'Kings Town', 1820/1828, artist unknown

After 31 January 1823, the official day of Governor Brisbane's abandonment of the breakwater project, the wall gradually began to fall into a state of disrepair. There was always an officially appointed harbour engineer whose duties included the maintenance of the breakwater, but during this period, little labour or funding was made available for the project other than for some minor repairs to the wall. In April 1824, an examination of the breakwater carried out by John Busby (1765–1857), the man who had been sent out to Australia to 'manage the Coal Mines', and who was now a government surveyor and civil engineer. Amongst other projects, John Busby is well remembered as the designer and supervisor of Sydney's first water supply. After his inspection of the breakwater, Busby's recommendation to Governor Brisbane was that in order to provide additional protection from the effects of the sea-swell on the vessels moored in the harbour, Newcastle's existing breakwater should be extended a further 75 yards towards the island. Busby promised to prepare an estimate of the costs of the work, but as no new work was initiated it appears that the Governor must have considered the costs too high.

As of 3 March 1824, Newcastle was opened to all free settlers, and it was from this date the nature of the small town rapidly changed from that of a penal settlement to one of a conventional colonial pioneer settlement. In 1823, in anticipation of the expected civilian expansion in the region, the government surveyor, Henry Dangar (1796–1861), surveyed and replanned the settlement. Dangar's official survey referred to the settlement of Newcastle as 'Kingstown'. Dangar, in his 1828 publication, *King's Town*, claimed that it was Governor Brisbane's express wish to honour the town's founder, Governor King, by having the town re-named after him. Regardless of whatever name was used, Newcastle threw off the shackles and accessories of a penal settlement and began its pursuit of a proper civilian destiny.

In order to gain a perspective of the living conditions in Newcastle after the lifting of strict military control, it should be noted that even by 1830 there were still only nine streets named, 192 building lots allocated and 40 not-so-grand houses constructed in the township. In comparison to the thriving metropolis of Sydney, Newcastle was very much still a bleak industrial and sea-faring village.

As the majority of Newcastle's convicts had been removed to Port Macquarie by 1823, and the original government purpose of establishing Newcastle as an exclusive penal settlement no longer applied, the government now found coal mining unprofitable and gladly relinquished its exclusive right to mine coal in the region, granting a monopoly on coal mining to the Australian Agricultural Company. Although this example of one exclusive body replacing another reflects the structure of power in the era, at least this introduction of private enterprise into the coal mining industry helped assure the necessity for, and future of, the port. The few remaining prisoners who were held in the stockade and who had formerly been employed in the coal trade were transferred to road and harbour improvements.

Although in terms of outgoing tonnage Newcastle's port has always exceeded Sydney's, before Newcastle became a free port with its own customs facilities, the cost of double-handling imported goods via Sydney was an unnecessary economic burden the region could ill afford and it could be argued that as an important and competitive port, the development of Newcastle had always been subjected to negative pressure from Sydney which retarded its development as a major trading centre. As most of the Hunter Region's prosperity was directly tied to the vagaries of sea transportation, the need for continuous improvement of harbour facilities was paramount to the future of Newcastle and the Hunter Valley.

Ultimately, the resumption of work on the breakwater's construction came about not because of any government initiative, but because of the agitation of citizens and private enterprise groups for improved and safer harbour facilities. They at least recognised that Newcastle Harbour's reputation as a safe and easy place to load the now burgeoning product range of the Hunter Region desperately needed enhancing. It was a fact that because of the dangerous harbour conditions that could be experienced, there was some difficulty for a ship owner in obtaining insurance for a vessel bound for the port of Newcastle, and this was a serious element that retarded overseas interest in using the port facilities.

Nobbys Island from Mullumbimba Cottage, 1830, artist unknown

There were other factors that influenced the resumption of work on the breakwater; among them, still the controversial issue of the height of Nobbys Island affecting the sailing ships entering the harbour, and the recognition of the need for an improved harbour navigational system. It had always been obvious that if Nobbys Island was cut down, the excavated material could be used to extend the breakwater directly from the island towards the mainland, yet it was not until 1832 that a select committee was formed to investigate the matter. Headed by the Harbour Master Captain Alexander Livingstone, the committee recommended to Governor Darling that the most desirable and practical solution to the problem of harbour safety was to lower the height of Nobbys Island and at the same time utilise the materials to continue the breakwater project that had been started by Macquarie and Wallis. From 1833 to 1836, any progress on the wall still remained inconsequential and the few records that survive today concerning the maintenance work that was carried out are sparse and vague.

Allocation of funds in small amounts can be traced, but any real advancement was negligible.

Work on cutting down the island and extending the breakwater began in earnest when the very able Captain George Barney became officially responsible for the construction of the breakwater on 9 June 1836. Captain Barney, accompanied by his family, had arrived in Sydney in December 1835 along with his detachment of Royal Engineers. Besides his military duties, Captain Barney was given the responsibility for important defence, navigational and civil works in Sydney, Wollongong and Newcastle. Although Barney did not reside in Newcastle, and at that time, he only delegated the supervision of work on the breakwater, a few years later his specific actions for a brief period in Newcastle's history would become extremely controversial, perhaps it could be said, even explosive. Given the availability of a work force of 200 convicts, Barney's initial estimate was that it would take five years from 1836 to complete the breakwater.

As most of the prisoners had been transferred from Newcastle to Port Macquarie long ago, the current convict workforce kept for public works numbered approximately only 80 men. They were known as the 'New Gang'. Using these men, work proceeded slowly. It was during this time that a small gang of prisoners was permanently stationed on the island, living in wooden shelters constructed on the southern side of the island. Evidence of these shelters can be discerned from some of the few early sketches of the island that have survived. Newly arrived prisoners allocated to the breakwater project were split into two groups — the Nobbys gang, being marooned on the island to work from that end, and the 'Chain gang' which worked from the southern end on the mainland. The chain gang resided in the old stockade.

George Barney

Since 1818, there had been no great improvements in building technology or techniques, and the work proceeded by hand as slowly as it had always done, with the convicts cutting down the island and using the material to extend the wall from the northern end and by excavating material from the Colliers Point Quarry to extend the breakwater from the southern end. To speed up the progress on the breakwater, some time in 1843, an additional 94 prisoners were shipped from Sydney accompanied by 27 soldiers. Of the 94 prisoners, 20 were sent out to work on the Nobbys end and the rest worked on the mainland. This took the total number of prisoners working on the project to approximately 180, and as far as it is possible to determine, this was probably the largest number of men ever allocated to the project.

One of the problems that had plagued the project from the beginning was that the materials being used on the breakwater were not ideal for the purpose. From the Collier's Point end, from both sides of the hill, soft sandstone rocks and rubble were still being taken to the extremity of the wall in primitive handcarts. It has been suggested that in this time a rail system was constructed from the quarries to the face of the breakwater and it has been claimed that a hand push rail system was built around both sides of the headland. There is no evidence to support the idea of a rail system before the late 1840s and available drawings only show the railway as ever having been on the seaward side.

By the 1840s the main quarry was on the seaward side of what is now Fort Scratchley, approximately opposite and just west from where Newcastle baths are today. In this period, the men were cutting and handling large stones that weighed approximately two tons each approx. (size about 0.9 of a cubic metre). These stones were loaded onto carts by the convicts with the aid of derricks and clamps and the carts were then pushed down hill to the extremity of the breakwater. From the quarry to the start of the breakwater the road formed a steady downwards incline and this would have substantially aided the carting of the rock. Some of the original road from the quarry to the wall cut into the side of the hill is still visible above the current seaward side esplanade. On 30 June 1843, a report of progress was submitted by Barney to the Public Works Department showing the progress of the breakwater as its being extended to 570 feet from Nobbys and 1290 feet from the mainland. This left a gap of 827 feet to complete the wall.

Environmental considerations which would certainly be of major worry to us today certainly did not seem to be an issue in the 19th century, for all through the era there was no concern or specific plan for the final shape of Nobbys Island, and even the ultimate determination of the island's exact height and its aesthetic appeal for a long time seems to have been of no consequence to anybody. It seems also strange, even today, that excepting for Macquarie's earlier mention in his diary of 'This most arduous and Herculean undertaking' that the scope and enormity of the task has never really been recognised. The difficulty in completing this incredible enterprise is never mentioned in any available correspondence from either the convicts or the government, yet using only hand tools the magnitude of the work must have been enormously daunting to all involved on the project. Perhaps the basic pioneering spirit of our forebears was simply a part of their stoic character?

Barney's original calculation of five years proved to be somewhat ambitious; it took over ten years to finally complete the wall. Considering the size of the project and the number of people involved in it, there is very little information available that allows an accurate analysis of progress, and this seems to reflect not only the colony's disinterest in the work, but somehow, also the apathy of residents of Newcastle towards the project as well.

Conrad Martens, circa 1841

The official day of the completion of the breakwater was 9 June 1846. The fact that there was no fanfare of any sort and that the event rates hardly a mention, seems paradoxical, and to be at odds, with the original ceremony of Governor Macquarie's inauguration of the project, a project for which he had so much hope. The last stones were put into place by the convicts and the first person to walk across the now completed breakwater was the current Clerk of Works, Mr Walter Scott. Local legend has it that, just before the last stones were tipped into position, to the cheers of the convicts, a fisherman sailed his vessel on a wave through the final gap in the wall. The story seems unlikely but it adds a pleasant touch to a significant occasion. Certainly after 28 years of servitude, the breakwater deserved some sort of grand finale.

Once again there was a period of little development or activity on the breakwater and for three years the structure suffered the ravages of the sea. The beach had not yet built up along the wall and the relentless action of the waves on the inferior building materials caused the wall to continually be breached by the sea. The wall was especially vulnerable at the narrowest section near the island. In 1849 it was reported that the wall was almost impassable and was broken in no fewer than nine places. From 1846 to 1853 the government continued to maintain 70 convicts at the old gaol to provide the labour for road and harbour improvements. Still cutting down Nobbys Island to obtain the material for the repairs, the government continued to carry out maintenance on the wall using the labour of these prisoners. Remarkably, enthusiasm for the original purpose of cutting down the island to reduce its effect as a windbreak had simply dissipated in the past 14 years.

On 7 June 1849, the Colonial Secretary advertised in the New South Wales *Government Gazette*, calling for private tenders to be submitted to carry out repairs to the wall, but there is no record of any tender being accepted by the government. This perhaps suggests that the labour of convicts was still the most economical option for maintenance. At this time the man in charge of maintaining the breakwater was an engineer named Captain John Edward Bull (1806–1901). Captain Bull was a man well respected not only for his contribution towards road construction in the colony, but also for his humanitarian attitude towards convicts. As an officer on the goldfields of Ballarat he recognised the injustice of the controversial gold tax and was one of the few bureaucrats that was sympathetic to the problems of the diggers. As revealed in his monthly report of April 1850, Captain Bull made plans to strengthen the structure:

> The mining and getting of stone at Nobby's continues to be worked by ten men throughout the month; and when the railway is laid down, which is now being prepared. The retaining wall alluded to in last report is finished and has so effectively strengthened the breakwater for about 40 yards that I intend to commence one throughout the narrow part, if approved of.

Whether it was because of the breakwater's proximity to shipping and hence the perceived opportunity for prisoners to escape by sea, or whether it was simply the fact that the breakwater was a restricted prison project, any person not directly employed on the project, citizen or convict alike, could be arrested if found near the work. On 13 September 1849, a curious act was passed by the Legislative Council that gave a clear warning to anybody not connected with the breakwater and Nobbys to stay well away from the area. It read:

> His Excellency the Governor directs it to be notified, that the Breakwater at Newcastle and Nobby's Island have been appointed places at which Male Offenders under order or sentence passed in pursuance of the provisions of an Act of the Governor and the Legislative Council, passed in the eleventh year of Her Majesty Reign, instituted, "An Act" to substitute other punishments for Transportation "Beyond the Seas" shall be detained, and be liable to be kept to hard labour.
>
> His Excellency also directs it to be notified, that under the provisions of the said Act, any person found at or near, or in any manner communicating with the said Breakwater or Island, without the permission of the Governor or proper Officer, will be guilty of a misdemeanour, and on conviction, be liable to a fine or penalty of 20 pounds, or imprisonment for three months, or both, of which all persons are hereby required to take notice.
>
> By His Excellency's Command
> E. DEAS. THOMSON.

After 30 years of construction, the breakwater still remained a desperate place for desperate men. For about three years there were no improvements made on the wall, with only the usual basic maintenance being carried out by convict labour.

As each difficult metre of this important project continued, the significance of the vision of Captain Wallis and Governor Macquarie seems to disappear into some pragmatic industrial haze. Somehow the story of Macquarie's Pier and Nobbys just limps along in the history of Newcastle, with the original essential hope and vitality of the project ever receding. Fortunately, to liven its history up, the next stage in the life of Nobbys would prove to be the most controversial and interesting, and whether fact or fiction, the 'blowing up' of Nobbys, even after a hundred years, is still a great yarn and at least ensures Nobbys' place in local history.

CHAPTER 6

The Blowing-Up of Nobbys Island

The present distinctive profile of Nobbys Island has become the symbol of the Hunter Region and it is not only well known to people throughout the country, but indeed to many thousands of mariners that ply the seas around the world. Although the sight of Nobbys Island evokes a certain amount of sentimentalism in Novocastrians, the island's current physical shape is clearly man-made and the direct result of colonial pragmatism. With the immediate needs of the pioneers of Australia being cardinal, it seems that the destruction and heritage value of this original sculpture of nature was never an issue in colonial times. Aesthetics were of little concern to our forebears. Before it was cut down the shape of Nobbys Island was symmetrical, and although it eventually would be so again; the condition of the island between 1846 and 1854 left much to be desired. The landfall which was the herald to Newcastle's arriving sea-borne guests had been reduced to, and left as, an unsightly inverted quarry, the appearance of which resembled an ugly lop-sided two-tiered wedding cake. The indiscriminate quarrying of the island had rendered it completely unrecognisable from its original and natural shape.

One of Newcastle's most interesting and controversial stories begins in the mid-1850s, that of the 'blowing up' of Nobbys' Island. The tale has progressively been told and retold, printed and reprinted so many times that the facts have become almost secondary to what is now one of Newcastle's best loved myths. Never let it be said that Novocastrians would ruin a good yarn by confusing the issue with the truth; yet even after all the facts are correlated and the story made plain, it is not too difficult to believe that 'it nearly happened'.

For 20 years, the need for a modern lighthouse and an updated navigational system for Newcastle Harbour was apparent to all, yet it was not until 1852 that any positive action was taken. As was usual for the era, a select committee was appointed to investigate the question of remedying Newcastle's problem of living with an antiquated harbour signal system. It was written in the report that:

> ... inasmuch as the trade of the port has increased during the last two years to a considerable extent, it is of the greatest importance that the present insufficient and frequently useless substitute, which is merely a heap of ignited coal on the Signal Hill, should be replaced by a substantial light on the Nobby rock.

John Hardwick, circa 1853

The idea of utilising Nobbys Island as a lighthouse site was not new. For many years, the old coal-fired beacon on Signal Hill (Fort Scratchley) had been recognised as an antiquated and inadequate signal system for the busy port of Newcastle. A government survey completed on 17 July 1851 by Captain John R. Stokes R.N. of the *Acheron*, resulted in the proposal for a new light being formalised. In 1852, a select committee under the chairmanship of Captain King R.N. was appointed to officially investigate the matter of a new light system.

There were two controversial questions which would generate enormous concern for Novocastrians: (a) the height to which Nobbys Island should be reduced, and (b) the best way to accomplish this. This community anxiety would lead to a response from what would prove to be Newcastle's first environmental action group.

The select committee sought advice from Captain John Bull (Army), the superintendent in charge of maintaining the breakwater at that time. Drawing on his experience of working with materials from the island in the past, Captain Bull's recommendation was to cut the island down to a height of 92 feet. At this level, all of the conglomerate and coal seams would be removed to leave a solid shale base on which a medium sized lighthouse could be built, finishing at a total height of one hundred and forty two feet above sea level. The select committee chose to ignore Captain Bull's advice and their final recommendation to the Government was to reduce the island to a height of 65 feet, opting for a lower base and a higher tower.

Naturally it was assumed that convict labour from the breakwater stockade (the old gaol) would be used. The then superintendent of the breakwater gang, Major McPherson, when asked about the labour, advised that even with the recent arrival of an additional 60 new prisoners, he could only spare 30 men for the specific task of cutting down the island. It was estimated that it would take three years to complete the work. The Colonial Secretary referred this report to the Chief Commissioner for Crown Lands, George Barney.

As an ex-Lieutenant-Colonel of the Royal Engineers, Barney was familiar with the breakwater project. He had served with the Royal Engineers in Australia in numerous influential positions which had included the maintenance and construction of port facilities in Newcastle in 1836. Other important military and civil works previously carried out by Barney were the constructions of Circular Quay and Fort Denison in Sydney. Barney sold his commission in 1846 but had returned to civil service in 1847 to serve as the superintendent in charge of establishing a new penal settlement at Port Curtis in Northern Australia. Unfortunately, the venture quickly failed due to the unbearable tropical conditions of the region. Barney had been elected as a member of the Legislative Council and in 1849 was appointed as the Chief Commissioner of Crown Lands. When the Colonial Secretary referred the matter of cutting down Nobbys Island to Barney, he also inquired if the work might be expedited by the use of gunpowder. The advocation of the use of gunpowder to blow the top off Nobbys was not new, it had been suggested as early as 1826 and once again in 1847 by Mr Lamb, a member of the current select committee. Barney adopted the idea with enthusiasm, and accompanied by a civil engineer, Mr G. K. Mann, and acting under the Colonial Secretary's instructions, they inspected the site and prepared a report. The report included the estimated cost of reducing the island at £1,002/11/6, a cost which included the supply of 17 tons of gunpowder.

By April 1853, Barney had the convicts digging galleries to accept the explosives. It is the mechanics and theory of Barney's design for the reconstruction of the island that continues to cause confusion and contention, and it is because of the enormous furore caused by the proposal at the time that, even today, the subject is still often debated. Opinion on the circumstances that surrounded the proposed use of explosives is usually split into two factions. There are those who believe that what was never understood by the agitators against the imminent explosion, was that Barney, at no time, ever intended to level the island with his 17 tons of gunpowder; and those who believed that he was going to blow the little island off the map! What is known is that his plan was to drive four tunnels into the island, one of which he intended to drive at almost sea level to the centre of the island from the seaward side (this tunnel still exists), and three somewhere else (positions still unsubstantiated). The known tunnel is still a source of historical argument. This tunnel was still visible and accessible in the 1920s, and even though its entrance is now covered by falls of loose shale, photographic evidence from the 1920s makes the position of the entrance easily locatable.

Explanations denying that this tunnel was Barney's work abound. Over the years articles have been written suggesting that the tunnel was an early coal mine, yet no coal seam exists at that level. Another explanation is that the tunnel was dug to provide shelter for the prisoners engaged on working on the Nobbys end of the breakwater. However, considering the tunnel's exposure to the prevailing weather and the extreme difficulty and impractical method of construction for this specific purpose, it seems an unlikely explanation. Unfortunately, because of the scarcity of records from the time, any complete picture of Barney's purpose and progress is difficult to ascertain, and the exact circumstances are not entirely clear. However, at the time of the impending explosion the subject certainly generated a substantial response from the local citizens, so much so that on 21 June 1854 they were moved to hold a public meeting in the old courthouse. The residents then petitioned the Colonial Secretary, expressing their fears about the effects that the imminent explosion might have on their properties.

By now, well aware of the state of agitation amongst the local citizens, the Colonial Secretary wrote to the inhabitants of Newcastle, his letter dated 31 December 1853, explaining that:

> ... it appears to his Excellency that you are under a misconception as to the nature or results of the work in progress for reducing the height of Nobby's Promontory, and which will neither have the effect of destroying the shelter now afforded to vessels entering the port during southerly gales, nor of obstructing the entrance, as is feared by you.
>
> The entire removal of Nobby's is not intended by the government, as seems apprehended by you; it is only proposed to cut it down to sixty five feet above high water mark, a height which is considered most advantageous for the base of a lighthouse, proposed to be erected thereon.

So George Barney was forced to clarify his proposal in detail. His explanation was that he had never intended to demolish the island entirely, rather, the explosion would cause the island to collapse on itself, leaving a base for the proposed lighthouse at the recommended height of 65 feet and at the same time blowing the excess material out to sea. Even allowing for the fact that Barney was an experienced engineer, his proposal would seem to be a very delicate and ambitious piece of engineering.

On 14 June 1854, the entire proposal involving Nobbys was discussed in the Legislative Council, including the estimate of the cost of materials required for the 'demolition' of Nobbys. Sir Charles Cowper (1807–1875) also reported to the Legislative Council on the same day that all chambers (note plural, but unfortunately he did not mention how many) were ready for the demolition of Nobbys. The *Sydney Morning Herald* reported on 22 August 1854, that Barney had completed three of the proposed tunnels, having driven them into the rock as far as 77 feet.

The question remains, given the enormous extent of Barney's autonomy and power, what was his original intention? And when called to account, was Barney's explanation satisfactory or was it a politic move to diffuse the embarrassing situation that had arisen for the government? History has accepted that it was never Barney's intention to annihilate the island.

Recently recorded direct anecdotal evidence from an elderly Newcastle resident indicates that there were at least two galleries driven into the centre of the island, both just above sea level. There was the known tunnel and another located on the south-eastern side of the island. Off the eastern most gallery is supposed to be an offset chamber measuring approximately three metres by three metres, and off the south-eastern tunnel are two chambers of the same dimensions, these chambers were presumably excavated to accept the explosives, the rooms being offset to diffuse the explosion. Although it would be possible, to date, this evidence has not been physically substantiated.

On 30 December 1853, Barney submitted a report stating that two galleries had been driven into hard rock to distances of 77 and 79 feet respectively. If it were possible to prove that the tunnels at sea level and the tunnels he reported on were one and the same, Barney's engineering technique would take a lot of explaining. Perhaps the Ex-Royal Engineer, Lieutenant-Colonel George Barney, with his 17 tons of gunpowder was denied a latent desire to be remembered for a spectacle that the colony would have long remembered, Newcastle's very own Krakatoa. Fortunately, for whatever reason, the decision to use explosives was rescinded. George Barney was appointed later as Surveyor-General for the colony, and he died on 16 April 1862. He is buried in St Leonards cemetery.

CHAPTER 7

The Finish

'The Nobbies from Newcastle', Frederick Terry, circa 1853

The success of the local resident action group in having Barney's controversial plan stopped heralded the end of the era of Newcastle being a place to which convicts could be transported. In July 1855, under the command of Major MacPherson, the 'breakwater gang' was transferred to Cockatoo Island in Sydney Harbour, ending not only the 37 year relationship between Macquarie's Pier and the convicts, but of half a century of continuous convict influence on the region.

As previously recommended by Captain Bull, the government eventually decided to reduce Nobbys Island to the height of 92 feet, instead of the proposed height of only 65 feet. This was carried out by private contract. A Hunter River railway engineer, Mr Wright, agreed to finish cutting down the island and to prepare a level surface for the proposed lighthouse. The work was started early in 1855 and completed on 11 July 1855.

The beaches alongside the breakwater that are so familiar to residents today, had not yet formed along the wall and, once again, because of the constant action of the sea on the soft building materials, the condition of the breakwater quickly began to deteriorate. Early in 1856, the government harbour engineer, Mr O.E. Moriarty, contracted out to Messrs Robson and Wood the task of reinforcing the breakwater. For the very first time in the history of the breakwater project, paid civilian labour was used to maintain the wall. Still winning material from the old convict quarries behind Fort Scratchley, and using the old rail system around the seashore, the private contractors strengthened the wall by conveying along the old rail line as much as 152 tons of rock per day.

In an attempt to stabilise the breakwater, two stone groynes were constructed. These groynes were simply rock walls built at right angles from the breakwater on the seaward side. The theory, which had been proposed by Colonel Barney in 1850, was that if the groynes were extended approximately 100 feet at right angles to the wall, a beach would build up around them and protect the wall from the ravages of the sea. The project initially met with some success, but eventually repeated gales destroyed both the beaches and the groynes.

In the 24 April 1857 issue of the *Government Gazette* the Colonial Architect invited interested parties to tender for the construction of a new lighthouse and keeper's residence on Nobbys Island. The new structures were duly completed, and at noon on 30 December 1857, the 36 year old coal-fired beacon on Signal Hill was extinguished and the new modem catoptric light on Nobbys Island was commissioned. The tower was 33 feet high, putting the light at 125 feet above sea level. The first lighthouse keeper was Mr Jesse Hannell.

From 1869 to 1872 the entire original convict-built breakwater was reinforced to such a degree that it was virtually rebuilt. A much more suitable stone cut into blocks weighing as much as 10 tons each were transported direct by steam train from the Waratah quarry to Macquarie's Pier. Although the original convict project still forms the foundation of the breakwater that exists today, absolutely no tangible evidence of convict influence can be seen.

There are no less than 25 streets around Newcastle named in Governor Lachlan Macquarie's honour, but despite the fact that even though most citizens of Newcastle may at least be vaguely aware of who he was, few today recognise the name

'Macquarie's Pier'. Paradoxically, Nobbys or Nobbys Breakwater, a name which to date remains devoid of a known origin, is completely familiar to the same residents. Relative to some public works projects, such as the multi-lane freeways, massive dams and bridges that are enjoyed by the community today, the breakwater was a simple construction. Yet imagine the reaction of the public today if a bureaucrat, acting on his own authority, suddenly committed the community to embark on a project that was of inestimable but certainly incredible expense, that would involve the winning and shifting by hand hundreds of thousands of tons of rock, that would consume three million man hours and take nearly forty years to complete. What a reaction would there be! The purposes of the projects were purely pragmatic, but for any person that has walked Macquarie's Pier and is now familiar with its story, they may sense that the enterprise has a presence that transcends its function as just a pile of rocks to protect the harbour.

It is unfortunate that, as inheritors of the region, we can never really know, in human terms, what the real cost of carrying out these two ambitious projects was. But hopefully, the legacy of the past endeavours of the early residents of Newcastle that are so well enjoyed by the people of Newcastle today are appreciated for what they once were — the vision of a dedicated few, paid for by the incredible labour and suffering of many.

... until history reveals more.

www.ingramcontent.com/pod-product-compliance
Ingram Content Group UK Ltd.
Pitfield, Milton Keynes, MK11 3LW, UK
UKHW041838200726
13854UKWH00003BA/1194